Syzygy, Beauty

···········

T Fleischmann

an
essay

Sarabande  Books

LOUISVILLE, KENTUCKY

Managing Editor
Sarabande Books, Inc.
2234 Dundee Road, Suite 200
Louisville, KY 40205

Library of Congress Cataloging-in-Publication Data

Fleischmann, T., 1983–
Syzygy, beauty : an essay / T Fleischmann.
     p. cm.
ISBN 978-1-936747-26-9 (pbk. : alk. paper)
I. Title.
PS3606.L453S98 2012
814'.6—dc23

                                        2011030324

Cover photograph: *Crystal Cottage,* by Benjy Russell.
Cover and text design by Kirkby Gann Tittle.

Manufactured in Canada.
This book is printed on acid-free paper.

Sarabande Books is a nonprofit literary organization.

NATIONAL
ENDOWMENT
FOR THE ARTS

This project is supported in part by an award from the National Endowment for the Arts.

The Kentucky Arts Council, the state arts agency, supports Sarabande Books with state tax dollars and federal funding from the National Endowment for the Arts.

Syzygy, Beauty

There are many things about you that people don't notice because you are pretty. Like that you are quickest to anger with people you love and that you are a perfect mathematician. Tell me who gave you that ring that swirls into its silver self. A shotgun wedding without a shotgun and a shotgun wedding without a bride are still excuses for two people to stand beside each other. In the morning I will lie beside someone that I love and you beside someone that you love, but when the day comes each person goes where they have to go. "I'm not as beautiful as you are tonight," I say, but only when I can't stop myself, my veil askew. It is god that makes someone a saint—all the church can do is recognize that person. Who am I to know the methods of something holy? The first thing I noticed about you was your lips and you were speaking.

A herd of gazelles will often measure five thousand. During mating season, the throats of male Mongolian gazelles swell as they bellow long loud bellows. Gazelle fur lines Meret Oppenheim's *Object*: a teacup, saucer, and spoon, suggesting a feminine sexuality present in every common object. She called her work "an enormously tiny bit of a lot." Sometimes two objects become one object, not as a hybrid or a duality but as a new thought that consumes both. In Mongolia a herd of gazelles numbering a quarter million runs across treeless fields, throats filled with the sound of desire. They are so numerous, the scientists say, that it is impossible to tell if they are dying and should be considered endangered. I found a way to give and take at the same time and with that new thought I approached you.

When you came to the mountain farm my legs were rashed red by chiggers and the sun slipped quickly behind the ridge. Soon, your tent was empty and you were in my bed, the hills cupped around us like hands taking water to a mouth. Water trickling down forearms. These days, at discos with my whiskey, I dance to hip hop like a riot girl and am never taken home. It was while dancing that I met my last boyfriend. "Don't you know anything?" he asked, sincere with frustration. "You're supposed to give me your number." I can't decide if it was all scripted, if you hopped the train that brought you south so we could meet. I've learned this lesson so many times before but it still seems as unheard as the birds, high and imperceptible above us.

By describing something we place it at a distance. My body is a fleshy thing, my body is tall and filled with citrus. I want everyone I have touched to send me a postcard on which they describe their fingers, but mostly I want them to do this before I have the chance to ask. At night, my eyes are unable to understand depth. When I was young I climbed a tree playing flashlight tag. I sat in it so long I forgot how high I was and leapt to get down, the earth like a flat punch as I tumbled to my ribs. I write down 102 words that say what I see when I see you, how it is a flat punch to look at you. How does it feel to know you are something I look at? In the morning, dress yourself in the clothes I removed last night.

Dim snow. Light tower. Peninsula. Skyscapes before
skyscapes. You say a ghost is an impression, like wet paper
in our hands. The white and blue of winter. The white and
blue of windows. An arm's distance as far as I can see.

I am having trouble living somewhere, or anywhere. After only a month has passed, I find myself on the side of the road again, walking to the trains. I have been so many places I must be sunlight. I have been diffused by clouds. To hike to the top of the mountain, I must spend the afternoon facing the steep slant of earth, my hands in brambles. Only once I am high enough can I turn and see the tin roofs and straight beds of flowers, dropped to a Euclidian flatness. Where have I been? Listen, I have been diffused by clouds, by everyone who has touched me, and just like you I am a radiation destined for the earth.

When I am not in the country I am in the city, so why not
your city, after all? A girl I sometimes date lives here, three
friends from college. Everyone is speeding beneath the
pavement, a rumble in tunnels we trust not to cave in. I walk
around with a basket of apples, unaware that apples are
out of season. I am suggesting that you bite the loaded
image, am calling myself a witch, a snake-devil. It's not tart
because of poison, it's just a tart apple. "You don't have to
trick me into hanging out with you," my friend claims. "Just
let me know what time." They say you have to live here for
ten years before you live here, so really this isn't any more
your home than it is mine.

See through mesh. Of all the *Cells* Louise Bourgeois made,
I stood before *Cell (Glass Spheres and Hands)* the longest,
a date at the Guggenheim ending. It is a cage of square
glass. Inside, large crystal balls sit on wooden chairs and
hands rest on the table. The walls announce an outside
and an inside, somewhere that I am and somewhere that I
am not. Touch is the conclusion of sight, and so Bourgeois
places the folded hands there, behind the glass. Your
clavicle dips so slightly down, then up again. A cage also
suggests danger, makes the natural curiosity of looking a
risk. To see an object, to consider its surface and texture,
is to ignore all else. "What does your boyfriend say about
me?" I turn to face you and ask.

It must have felt, after you won the tiara, like someone had slathered you with papier-mâché. Let's use your form to gather rain and the rain will deflate the form. If you go to see the ancient drawings in the Lascaux caves, you will instead see identical drawings two hundred meters away. Someone enters once a month to undo the damage our breath, rich with carbon dioxide, has caused. Ask her if there is any difference between one bull and its twin. What makes the images impressive is the use of movement and perspective, the possibility of sky charts. The point where two railroad tracks come together is the point where they vanish, one new thought that leaves our sight. I could see you better if you were to lie down and touch your fingertips to each other like an arrow, your form a flower trough.

Your boyfriend and I are going to mingle, to cross-pollinate and appropriate. You are going to flit between us until I say his "Oh boy!" and he bites his lip like my bottom lip. And the King ordered you cut in two, so that one half could be given to me and one to your boyfriend. And I said I wanted the half with your firm butt, which was just as well, as your boyfriend wanted the half with your pretty face. In mathematics a knot is different than the knot on a sail or shoelace because it has no ends and so cannot be undone. The string of the trefoil knot spins around itself forever, three loops in one form. Three people holding hands can dance and dip, taking turns being held, leaning back without falling. Severed, the trefoil knot becomes a line that ends, a segment.

Spirit catch of breath. Appellations tumble off your lips. You tell me and you tell me again. I still want to talk about it, the ice breaking and water seeping out. The pain in my lungs. Your lips.

To be honest, I don't find your boyfriend attractive, not
really, although I won't tell you that. I find something very
small, you say, and make it to be something very large.
The lens of the projector and the bodies on screen, like
the difference between who he could be and who he is.
Leaping to touch the light (shadows). Proximity offers a
certain beauty, makes the glass orbs be more than crystal
balls. It's a given that you're desired, the way you pull off
that flannel shirt. Me, I have to pin a tulip to it. Me, I have
to study the part in everyone's hair. I throw a crystal ball
into the air and still some light shines through, obscures the
screen. She must do something right if he's dating her.

When the company left we would take turns, one of us
washing the dishes and the other washing their face. Two
rooms whispering with water, like we lived together. Tracey
Emin's *Everyone I Have Ever Slept With, 1963-1995* is a
blue tent with 102 names appliquéd to the inside fabric.
On the floor it says, "With myself, always myself, never
forgetting." Sleep, which is what she means, listing her
grandmother and her twin, her lovers and the two fetuses
she aborted, all the intimacy sewn like patches. If we lived
in a nylon home the rain would sound much louder and I
might not hear you in the morning. Such a thin divide when
there are so many people in the world, all enraged by your
pretty fingers. You and I try to find ways to be alone, the
guests gone and the wallpaper only names. Place any two
things in a dome and still they will not be the same thing,
just together.

Not living anywhere, there is always the chance that I will leave and the chance that I will come back. From one coast to the other and here again, a different ragged route each time. When you walk me to the train, my purse loose in your hand, I am hoping you will ask me to stay. I am hoping to show grace when I tell you I can't. In a field in Michigan, the dead dry grass is in a permanent sway, pointing the way the snow drifts. Digging down until the earth is cold, then further, where it is warm. Once a song begins, the moments before each string is plucked are as filled with music as the moments after, silent and alive. "Didn't you just leave?" a friend will ask when I return to the city.

Oppenheim was so known for her teacup that barely
anyone noticed she kept living and making. She had been
photographed nude, fucked famous men. Critics debate if
this was a collaboration, where between subject and object
she stood. Aflight, I remember our dates in the mountains,
what you told me about construction, when cedar was
appropriate and when poplar. We danced because we
both knew the same dances, your friend condensing
his accordion. When you held my arms to the bed I felt
like a femme fatale who could swing a hammer, and no
matter how many times we touched, you stayed gorgeous
and I stayed me. For years, Oppenheim was depressed,
unrecognized. It was when she presented drawings of her
hands that the weight of youth began to lift.

Scratched film. Lit scrim. A forest is nothing but thousands of trees blocking each other from our view. Something to sleep under. Imperfect as bark.

If I turn and stand and face the projector, the ending image
won't be shadowed, the light too high above me. My friend
is afraid of the open sea, so I take him around a pond in
a paddle boat. "No, this is good, this is good," he says.
It is necessary to encounter very small things before we
approach something very large. We cannot be partners
because you have a partner and I have to leave. We're
just spending time together. I can sew a robin's egg back
together and you will treasure the care in its construction
despite the hollow body. You can build a second moon and
I will treasure the balance of gravity it destroys, nothing
floating like it used to. The darkness of the theatre allows
touch and the people of the theatre prevent it. The surface
of water will always break, but if you come at it from high
enough, it will break you back.

The vase is a classic form. Grayson Perry's *Golden Ghosts* is a pot, pale and purple-bruised. Children, a dog, and a teddy bear float gray and flat before a background of stenciled cottages. Perry is there many times, too. He is drawn in gold lines, presenting as Claire, his other self who wears dresses that poof. The body is a classic form, meaning the body is something we should understand, but have not yet managed to. I lift your shirt and write "I love you" on your stomach. I turn you over and write "I love you more" on your back. I'll place you like that on a pedestal, your neck relaxed and the lilacs in your mouth. We are only supposed to be pretty in a very particular way, and if we are pretty in a different way, the public will be made uncomfortable. After many years of watching them, people are able to identify wild birds by their silhouettes.

Above us, arboreal life. Imagine everything you have done
and you never bothered to touch the earth. A mobile draws
attention to floating movement, seeking an equilibrium upset
by the constant shifts of the world. A lesson for children,
laying them in their cribs to watch how restlessly everything
turns above. When we return to the hollow, we will
watch the sharp rise of trees on either side, the fireflies so
numerous and high they seemed to be a continuation of the
stars. I'm afraid that if you and I stop and are still you will
notice me, so I put my body on top of yours and breathe.
My rhythm on your rhythm, steadying into each other,
no tent around us. When I first left the city, I couldn't stop
commenting on how bright it was, as though the moon and
stars were more startling than streetlights.

I have decided to build a house here, near the houses where my friends live and across the creek from where my friends camp. It does not mean that I am staying, just that I want two small rooms, sometimes. A porch wrapped in screen. A friend of mine tells me she has a glass curse, that it came after she lit religious candles she knew nothing about. The glass that held the wax cracked, and then all her glass kept breaking, falling or being taken, suddenly, by a thin and crooked line. As far as I remember, I have been waiting for my life to come together, those pieces to settle until I am there. So many moons off which you can reflect to me. "I didn't," my friend says, "expect the curse to follow me out of Brooklyn."

My hands weren't cold at all, but neither were your pockets warm. The wood stove puffing up the sky and the clouds gracefully coming at night to hold the sun's heat a moment longer. One way to knowledge is somatics, what the body tells us. Like I know you, like we're familiar. You lie curled into yourself, protecting your heart and your head from the rest of the world. I can stand behind you when you point straight ahead and still reach my fingertips to yours. The oldest mountains in the world, they say, if you don't count fields and oceans. To pause implies that it all has a reason. To expect warmth.

Call me the bowerbird, I'll make sure all the beetles are
near-colors and demonstrate discretion when picking up
stones. Which mate will show up? I'll dance and see. I'm
working these pants today, working my hair, that long
strand in the front that can go to either side. So many hours
carrying lumber and oh my, look at these arms. My craft
project is the one falling from the ceiling of third grade,
strips of glitter on the cute boy's desk. I have nothing
to wear to a wedding so good thing I don't believe in
weddings. If it's about charming then it's about being
earnest, not waking at dawn to find white feathers but
pumping my wings so hard when I see you.

I try to figure out the equations on scrap boards, digging
pen into wood. Rivulets of ink and dirt clogs. The more exact
the alignment, the easier this will be later on. There is a very
important part of your life into which I am not welcome.
Chairs not meant for anyone to sit on, that we are barely
allowed to see. All of it there to deprive me of green glass.
And then there are the parts of my life in which you are not
welcome, the spider web strands of thought and the rows of
Michigan corn. Houses as places to be safe, and hundreds
of little ones, again and again, even if we can't exit. I mark
thin lines to cut. Two boards aligned with the same board
will not always be aligned with each other, an angle for
water to catch and rot away.

It's very important to me that you wear those sunglasses that are blue plastic and shaped like hearts. They make you tilt your head and pout at first, but then you forget and scowl like you aren't wearing heart-shaped sunglasses. Maybe something has to be remembered to be true. My mother and her neighbor run into each other at the grocery store and talk about the lilac bush that suggests a border between their two yards. "Is it mine or is it yours?" and they both offer the blossoms to each other. At the end of the day, removing my clothes, every flaw is present again. I am a naked body and you are a naked body wearing shades. Were there no story of how we met we would have always known each other.

102 words written on the walls of our cave. I'll build us a house of paper, out of green glass, out of tin, out of string. Such flimsy barriers, and I'm on the next flight north. I need you to press my body against the corner where two walls meet so that I can feel like I am being embraced twice. The three of us in the corner where two things meet. For six days in 1994, anyone with a telescope could watch fragments of a comet collide with Jupiter in the form of twenty fireballs. At its closest, Jupiter is 390,000,000 miles from the earth. At its most distant, it is 576,000,000 miles away. It's amazing that we can't feel something so large coming and going. A mother moved her son out of my old apartment complex. She cried by the truck while he lifted boxes, his face blank. The atmosphere that protects the earth does not have an end point, but becomes thinner and thinner until it does not exist.

The opening sequence to *Mary Tyler Moore?* Don't mind if I do. Coffee that I didn't brew and the hundreds of us not looking at each other. I take care to turn off the lights while my date and I are still wearing tee shirts, keeping my chest anonymous. We're always hesitant when we make the private public, covering ourselves in fur and hiding behind a wall. But I go on dates just so I can talk about them. I place my hand on his lower back to say here, this is where you can place your hand. There are literally millions of people around us, distractions with homes. I smile and swing a purse and hope someone will ask me about my afternoon at the park. You'll show me your new apartment, and when we get ready for bed I'll wait, only taking off the clothes that you take off first.

I'll know your boyfriend by the arch of his back at your touch. You say that we can't recreate the film *Meat Joy* because we're both vegan, but I say that's not the point. I need to invite six of our friends over. I need to pour paint on our flesh so we are all the same perfect colors, slipping bodies. It's the only way to prove ourselves that I have left. Someone new again, I forget how quickly I can become someone new again. The days we didn't kiss flake off my shoulders like dried paint. The days you touched my hand flake off my shoulders. I'm facing a very real problem, enjoying the view from the edge of your life. But filmed touching, you and I will always be, like the way two syllables collapse into each other.

An occultation is when something passes between you and me and we cannot see each other. I am on one side of the moon and you are on the other. In order to see anyone, we have to accept that she will occult the background. So close to each other, you occult the tent, and if you were gone, the tent would occult the ash tree. When I talk to your boyfriend I try to look him directly in the eye. Sometimes doing this takes so much concentration I miss what he says and then I follow his expression, smiling if he is smiling and looking stern if he is looking stern. On the deck of the boat, anyone with a telescope could watch us breaking the atmosphere with our cigarettes, and if you look long enough at the background of Perry's vase you will notice that it is idyllic.

When a date asks me if I am single I say, "Oh, you know.
There's this person." I leave you as general and moth-thin as
possible, for once undescribed. You may as well be a room
with a shut door. Normally, you may as well be lips behind
lipstick. That is the room where we live now, the door shut
and some tramp imagining what is inside. A marriage
of fleeting conjecture, the courtship a race of Who Can
Buy the Most Drinks for the Most Pretty Ladies. Even god
can't really say what something is without burning stars.
When asked if you are single, I imagine you mention your
boyfriend.

Someone is walking down Broadway, looking pretty the way I am supposed to look pretty. I am going to buy her pink drinks, take her to a motel room, and cloy her into cutting my hair. On seeing Oppenheim's fur-covered bracelet, Picasso noted that you could cover anything with fur. I would cover anything with paper or blush, a tiny light atmosphere that clings to the surface. I would cover you with gauze so when we kissed we both felt gauze. We would always be a thread's width apart from one another, and the haze in your eyes would make me more beautiful. Peel back the fur, scrub away the glue, and you have a teacup that was once not a teacup. If I see you in fifty years I'll recognize you the way I recognize a saint, by the silhouette of your wild bird.

Tongue on palm. Finger curve. You move your open hands to suggest a hip, like you are summoning the future from a crystal ball.

I'll admit that I like to say "and his boyfriend" right after
I say "my boyfriend." And then sometimes I say "his ex-
girlfriend," too. What it implies about me. How modern we
are here with outfits like strings of light and no future. You're
busy rubbing your temple and I'm resting my cheek in my
palm, like oh my, how could this have happened. At the
karaoke bar later tonight you are going to point at me every
time the chorus comes back. I'll laugh at this and I'll have
your shirt on because the temperature dipped. Right now
we're eating lunch and when asked later how we spent our
day there won't be much of a story. The ginger sizzling in
the pan. I don't know the song you're humming. Here, taste
this.

If there were 102 of me, I would not be the most beautiful.
I would be the one with the swollen throat and the ragged
haircut. In *Golden Ghosts*, Claire wears her *Coming Out
Dress*, also made by Perry. In real life, it is silver-sleeked
blue with yellow faeries and pink imps embroidered onto
its sheen. It frills at the bottom and it frills at the top. Pretty
like a little girl, one of the ways we aren't supposed to be.
I will gather gauze around my waist and walk a catwalk,
demanding notice. The person I think I am will consume
the person I am, and the person walking will be neither of
us, not a centaur nor a griffin. The scrim behind me will be
backlit and I will foreground fog. On the vase, Claire is thin
gold lines, the only person you can see through.

And what would I do, were the walls not there? I doubt touch would be enough. I think I would need to take. In her diary, Bourgeois says, "I want to be transparent. If people could see through me, they could not stop loving me, forgive me." And so she made cells that you could not see through, forcing us to peek around a corner. It is very intentional, that I never apologize. I have no other choice but to go to Denver, where a boy on a couch will give me the eye. Had I not traveled south again, who would be stacking these split logs and yes, I knew the gala was this evening. The hands in Bourgeois' *Cell* are carved of marble, pink like flesh, which is perhaps anatomically obvious. It is exceedingly difficult, deciding when to be obvious and when obscure. But even if I were to mail you a stolen glass orb, I fear you would fail to notice the pale green tinge, its tendency to roll off the table.

Before setting in a mold, bronze will expand to fill the
smallest details. Before I knew you, I knew a wax version of
you, a hollow cast of you in paraffin, and a mold that was
the negative of you. I held them all in my arms and then left
them in the shop. I sought the smallest details, the lengths of
each eyelash long enough to note and the too high arch of
your feet. The details that only I and your boyfriend will see.
A wax copy shows the parting lines, where two sides of the
mold met imperfectly. To remove these lines you must run
hot metal over the seam. If you did this to me I would try not
to scream, but I would show the scar to all of our friends.
"This is where he tried to change me so that I couldn't forget
him," and they might finally realize what a god damn hero
I am.

There are thousands of lawns between us, and so thousands
of borders you must cross to reach me. Stand on each
one and throw flowers to the left and to the right. "Think
of it instead like you're on the same dirt," she tells me,
"and there aren't any borders after all." In the South Pole,
scientists bury a telescope the size of a cubic kilometer. It
detects the blue light that shines when a neutrino impacts
an atom of ice. As most neutrinos move through the
atmosphere unaffected, the telescope is using the earth to
filter the universe, catching what collides. This afternoon,
the plena music from a courtyard and the bitter taste of
lettuce impressed a blue light upon me. Keep measure of
everything I heard and dismissed and it will show that I
am not a transparent medium. They chose the South Pole
because they needed ice as old and tight as possible, free
of air.

The bodies in *Meat Joy* are ecstatic because they are
bodies, flailing and dancing together: I take the lesson to
heart. Some of us like to be objects, indiscernible under
paint. Some of us want to be used. I can't insist that you
stop smiling so god damn gorgeous just because of my
stained teeth, so I steal your lipstick instead. You and I and
your boyfriend have never been together. You have never
wondered if it was my thigh or his pressed against you,
your face in the pillow. Eve became holy when she brought
us knowledge, pointing to it dormant in our chests, just as
you will feel the rush of him through my touch, each of us
and each of us and each of us together. Schneemann says
it is the energy of the audience that gives power to each
element of the performance.

The reasons that I am not as pretty as you are so numerous it is hard to tell if they are endangered or not. My boots, for instance. And the effects of harsh lighting. While you are out I draw a line down the middle of your room, *Brady Bunch* style. Your bed and books here, my wig there. "No, look at me," is what I mean to say. A centaur looking over his shoulder is a pretty boy looking at a horse's ass, and if we died in an embrace paleontologists of the future might think we were of one body. My blank postcards and stencils to the left, your dirty teacup to the right, and lilacs a border between us. It all seems so effective until you return and remind me I don't live here.

The sky has always been above us, so we must have always wanted to touch it. The sea there, its sound saying "bend, draw your fingers like a rake." The boys that you remember, leaning against the railing. Your boyfriend in a glass cage like a glass orb.

There is a couple in your neighborhood, one who looks like me and one who looks like you. The you is wearing shorter skirts. The me is letting herself go. We can give every part of myself a name and then we can give it a counterpart. Once we gather all the parts and counterparts together, I will be divine. My compulsion to paint furniture is called "Agnes." Your habit of showering so long that water bubbles under the wall, we'll call that "Jacob." Agnes, Jacob. Jacob, Agnes. The pleasure is all mine. There is the world of light above us and the world of us below it. By perceiving we make our place imperfect, by looking at each quality and seeing only it, separate from our faults and our flings. Us is an entity that sleeps in the tickle of high grass.

"It's so much more fun to say 'hobgoblin' than to say
'goblin,'" I tell you. The insecure hobgoblin of my body. The
raging hobgoblin of *Vanity Fair*. You are too occupied with
the crossword puzzle to respond. Stressing my negative
qualities only seems like a good strategy for finding a
partner until I realize it's the same strategy teen girls use.
Next I'll be making fun of Becky's flat chest and stealing
jelly bracelets from The Icing just to say something about
myself. I admit that I'm growing exhausted with my efforts
to seduce your boyfriend, but the alternative is bleak and
away. Eight letters, the 1991 Pet Shop Boys single that
quotes *Othello*. You are in love and I am dropping pennies
in the space between, making my wishes plop.

I want to be entirely you and me, and I want to be nothing but you and me and him. I'm putting on my checkered dress tonight, my thighs smooth and high. You're helping me visualize the boy I'll bring home. The task at hand is to logic out the material, to understand what we are. My physics book as a holy text. For a photograph to give us an image, the silver of crystal must be developed, the image first fogged, then seen. The reds and blues decided by exposure and the silver washed away. The boy I bring home is not you, at least not yet. The colors in *Meat Joy* are so similar that it is sometimes hard to see who and what.

Louise Bourgeois' parents repaired tapestries, and at
a young age she learned to help them draw in missing
segments. At the time, her father carried on an affair with
her governess, and her mother used the girl to watch
them. Later, Bourgeois called this child abuse. Is there pain
inherent in loving two who do not love each other? I left
the city today and went out into the world, ready to make
everyone fall for me. I will move state-by-state, and when
I return, you will be powerless to the echoing desire in my
voice. For Bourgeois, the home is not a sanctuary, but an
enclosure for a very certain danger, a place where you risk
yourself. Existentially severed limbs. With a start, I realize I
may return to find you now have two boyfriends.

A dead field in Montana is white, like it's suggesting the
winter about to come. I watch it pass from a train that is
always on the same track. We have been on this train for a
very long time and still we have not reached a singularity.
I slept with so many beautiful people in the past, some of
whom would not have slept with you, no matter how you
begged. I once looked like a rock star in the morning,
and eventually, I am sure of it, someone is going to plant
me daylilies. Is going to think herself lucky. The idea of
the ghost is that, once we are dead, we return as pretty,
floating blue things, but everyone freaks out instead of
complimenting our sheerness. If your ex-boyfriends came
back and filled the room I would hope at least one would
compliment me (your boyfriend has never complimented
me). It's true, the sky in Montana is impossibly bigger than it
is other places. And so the mountains seem smaller, too.

The *Secret Book of John* describes the four heavenly powers
as understanding, grace, perception, and thoughtfulness.
Powers you can block with a wall, or by a lack of coffee. I
return south again because here it is quiet, I see each bud
come and know what winter does. I cut hundreds of boards
of rough cut poplar at the same angle. There is no one I
love here. It's possible that I'm overanalyzing, like you
suggest. That we're happy when we're together and that
being happy is something like a berry bush or the wine we
made from the berries. Berries and later wine. After several
hours of thoughtful countryside perception, I call you on the
phone to tell you that I feel like a swan in love with a plastic
swan.

Tintype true. Like there is no one here to see you. Like you are remembered and gray and yellow and easily damaged. Precious terror, and the process to know you are there.

How on earth do you expect me to be either of those things? How on the moon in a dress? How on the sun in a suit? Butterflies keep flying into the house I am building, attracted to the white-painted walls, and none of them know enough to leave, dead red wings on the white floor. It's bad enough that you're pretty. Your eyelashes, your fingers. The worst is that, if I tell you how horrible your prettiness is to me, I sound foolish, and no one wants to be an ugly fool. I'll just hold it inside like flapping dead wings. One day I'll open my mouth and nothing will fly out. It's not your fault that you fell in love with him first, that the world is so filled with boys and girls. All you're trying to do is kiss me as I rub my butterfly gut.

It's not crazy to think the letters of the newspapers, rearranged, might be a message meant only for one of us. I memorized the way he danced before he told me he copied the twist from his last boyfriend. You dance that way, too. Make a column of syllables and say them all at once, see what collapses like Babel, who is scattered over the face of the earth. The people you love are in so many different places, phone calls and postage away. I am here, the place where I sleep, and your boyfriend is there, the place where you sleep. Everyone else can hear what we said, but we can only hear the tones and whines with which we spoke. Perfect timbre, sung wordless across a hallway, is an argument against conversation.

Cell is absent a body, but there are the hands, and there is us on the outside, being bodies. Is it cruel to place touch at the center of a piece that forbids touch? Or are we made aware again of our eye's strength? Beauty is cruising, turning on the street and moving your chin down and up again. It's keeping everything so far away that we don't know how far away it is, and it's recognizing that something could be closer. I've had a thousand imaginary boyfriends and not a one of them has left me for you. When you leave me it will be for you. We can glimpse each other through *Cell*, glass blocks unable to fully occult.

"Is this about how you don't want to be a boy?" you ask
me. In *Strangeland*, Tracey Emin recalls an adolescence of
fucking and drinking. It is in three sections, "Motherland,"
"Fatherland," and "Traceyland," defining ourselves by the
names on our walls, then defining ourselves by ourselves.
One review suggested that "certainly some of it should have
been edited out by someone who loves her." There is no
difference between saying who we want to be and saying
who we are, and if I hate the body in the mirror all I need to
do is smooth my skirt and move on. "What I mean," you try
to clarify, "is that I don't think this is about me at all." Had
I wanted to eat the apple, I would have plucked it from its
high branch and chewed until I finally knew.

On *Golden Ghosts*, the teddy bear is gray, partially
overlapping Claire so that it blocks her gilded right arm.
When young, Perry's mother left his father for their milkman,
who likewise left his wife and another lover to be with her.
Perry retreated into his bedroom to hide from the violent
man, inventing a world with his teddy bear, Alan Measles.
The beauty of having a room is that, while hidden there,
we can imagine ourselves to be anywhere. The world not
around us, any world might be around us, and any version
of us in it. If you retreated into the hollow with me, the
mountains could be our walls and the branches boughs of
tomorrow. There would be no reason to imagine us apart.
Perry filled his room with very small airplanes. "I don't know
what my mother's motivation was for marrying my father:"
he later said, "perhaps she fell in love."

Let's go to where mail goes when it's in the mail, waiting to get to your house. When I mention I am going on a date you rarely seem to react. I try mentioning the date again, but still, nothing. Insecurity is wanting to buy you a gift that I don't buy. Instead of learning new languages so that we can all talk, why not just turn to silence as our commonality? Everyone silent together, hands on hands. Or speak every language at once, the chattered cadence leveling itself? While the letter made its way to your house, I busied myself with pancake-making and banjo music. I thought about whether you and I are destined and what for, and when the envelope arrived I felt a slight heft of responsibility shift, some dust rising.

Feather bed. Soft rise. The past made alight by impact, the cells settling softly. Nostalgia is so gray, asking us to return to when we met, when I was too shy to look at you.

"He is not," my friend reminds me, "your last boyfriend."
Yes, obviously, obviously. It should be so clear to her that
you are my last girlfriend, I wonder if I am representing you
wrong. You are not a gazelle but gazelles, choking with
desire for yourself. So god damn fit, I don't even know if
I love you. I want to ask Perry about his work. When he
is etching Claire again and again on a vase, is he doing
so as Claire, or as Grayson? Can that distinction temper
narcissism? T flying on their broken butterfly wings, all of
Montana beneath. Broken-winged T like a tragic Hummel
on a hill. Although he wore frocks most of his life, it wasn't
until adulthood that Perry took a photo of Claire. "I wasn't
sure if I was Grayson or Claire in the dress: many things,
'Claire' and 'transvestite' included, didn't exist until they had
a name."

Laying the foundation is the most difficult step. Measuring and leveling, again and again. Everything needs to be so certain. My body is not a male body except in the sense that it is male. The box I sometimes check. I look awful with long hair and all the best dresses dip in the wrong tight way. It's no different than everything else you know about me, still and glittering in the air. And even were I strong and clear, someone like a sky to fly in, I still know you saw me first down a path, thought a thin boy was shuffling toward you. I place cement blocks and above them I will place the floor, the walls, a place to stay.

"My friend is coming to visit," I tell my friends, meaning you. I hope it will be just like when we met, when you were too cute and then I got drunk. Emin's tent glows, the stitching like shadowlines in the light of it. She says she sews because she is good at it, not because she is "trying to come up with some kind of grand female statement." The subject of Emin's art is always herself. I take it as a starting point, sport a denim dress as I cut purlin strips for my roof. I'm not doing this for any other reason than to build a house in the Appalachians. It is not a Grand You Statement. Before you arrive I install two lights inside so it glows on the path, something you can walk toward if you forget your torch.

Before I described the house it already existed, I just had to say "house" to get my purchase on it, to flaw it with my vision. Once I named you "lilac" you became something I could pick, a panicle with many small blooms. This is the house where you don't live with me. Down the creek is another house where you don't live with me. My god, they're everywhere, these houses where you don't live with me. Speaking of her *Cells*, Bourgeois asks of pain, "When does the emotional become the physical? When does the physical become the emotional?" Her glass orbs are fragile, meaning vulnerable. If you stayed here I would say we were in a "garden," would suggest that we move to the mountains for good. When you introduce me you say I am your "friend," but with a pause, a hesitation while vocabulary spreads about.

At seventeen, Oppenheim wrote the equation $x = $ hare in
her math book. Gluing fur to logic, her answer spry as it
jumps away. There is imagination in truth, she knew, floating
with all the numbers that try to make the world one equal
thing. Woven bone forming after a fracture, the bits held
close before they are made stronger. Let's make gravity
equal to being stood up at the prom, and the imperceptible
speed of the universe can be the necessity of art. $Y = $ me,
my valiant insecurities. I am preoccupied, trying to saturate
the cosmos with my experience, and I do not notice that you
take my elbow and guide me. The river we walk toward has
been so many things, I don't know how we'll ever arrive.

People familiar with Oppenheim's teacup are most often familiar with Man Ray's photograph of the object. Oppenheim challenges utility, invites touch and repulsion in a lasting moment, and Man Ray takes a picture of it. A description of the bed you are building your boyfriend, the words you pick like pricks of light, so I can describe them as stars or just as pricks. Making things seems a much better strategy than talking about it all. But then, the ghosts are a pale block in our line of sight, and I doubt you'll hear what I say with so much wind in the lowered windows. With my hands on your sides I can lift you up, we're together and the action is the thing. Some critics point out that Oppenheim was busy making fetish objects, but they don't seem to realize she was calling Man Ray a spoon.

Staring at you is like swooping down and attacking, like I
leave the sky and am vulnerable, too. This has nothing to do
with you. You're asleep, your body bent around a pea. You
may as well be holding a mirror to me. "I'm only attached
to ideas so long as they're useful," you say of religion, and
I'm filled with a fever to remind you that nothing is truly holy.
White white wings on a white white dove, like I don't see
the collar feathers and eyes. One of the reasons the holy
cannot be known is that we note a flaw and a perfection
instead of the soaring, unnamed bird, the thousands of
running gazelles, the steaming ice. You wake up and I am
part of your day. There are 102 descriptions of you on the
wall:

You are very small and upside down.
You will soon be covered with frost that looks like lip gloss.
Your body is made of many V's.
You toss love like it will land in worn leather.
You are soft, your body.
Your throat suggests there is gold lamé inside of you.
You have eyelashes for days.
You fell from the sky and when you landed you took some
    earth with you.
You are going to break eventually, and then you will be
    shards of amber glass.
You are surrounded by pointing erections (which way to the
    bar? that way).
Your eyes are green.
You are waiting for me to forge something out of steel and
    to place it in your lap.
You are flaking off the gold of your outline.
You comb your hair with one of those black picture-day
    combs.
You groan apples that thud, thud on the ground.
You stole someone's blush.
You are prone to turning your back, which is your best
    feature.
Your teeth are white.

You tear paper.

You lie down on a pillow that is not as soft as you are.

Your eyelids are the shapes of two birds without heads.

You are always standing in front of the sky.

You look away just the moment after I think you will look
away.

You clear the gong out of your throat.

You must be drawn with a very fine pen.

Your bracelet is rational.

You are the recovered grace and cheekbones of old
magazines.

You have the natural scent of a pine tree.

Your habit is to pick up rocks and then drop them onto your
knee.

You laugh by opening your mouth and your eyes as widely
as you can and grabbing someone's hand.

You favor purple.

You walk slowly so other people feel like they are pulling
you along.

You are tan and it is not even spring yet.

You fall deeper asleep and relax, curving the curve of your
body into mine.

You only photograph in black and white.

You eschew cotton and leave the shower naked.

You are throwing leaves and hollering names.
Your lips part just enough to make them more pink.
You convince fireflies to stand still.
Your shirt cuffs are short and you pull them down.
Your sparkle is in your gut.
You made a promise to stay awake until I fell asleep and I
   hear that in your breathing.
You have one more crease in each palm than I do.
You have young cells.
You stand there and it's not a street corner anymore, it's
   someplace else.
You turn, with enough sun, to the color of bourbon.
Your hair flatters your forehead, the way it recedes.
You did not ask for any of this but are still dressing up.
You speak to me with a baritone voice, like your voice
   echoing in a baritone.
Your long game is your ab hair, your short game your scent.
You walk like a male cheerleader.
Your gaze wears brass knuckles to the bar.
You are waiting for winter, when you can pull your hood
   tight and I will still recognize you.
You make eyeshadow redundant.
You stopped before the shelf with the book in your hand
   and your arm raised just so.

Your ribs are exacting, asking for my tongue against them.
Your skin is the same all over.
You whippoorwill again and again on either side of my
　　sleep.
Your arms are the size to go around my chest, hands
　　clasping opposite elbows.
You wear it well (glitter).
You are the days and nights of some classic film star.
You have pores but no one can find them.
You lift the drink, begin to speak, set the glass on the table,
　　and are silent again.
Your gut is very, very soft and white.
Your calves are thicker than expected.
Your symmetrical bug bites.
You give the camera a look and the flash doesn't go off.
Your front teeth point toward each other.
Your eye is as full of the sky as the sky is.
Your hand does not smell like my hand.
You look good, everyone says, touching your arm.
Your thighs seem motionless when you walk away.
You are passionate in your shepherding.
Your paunch makes me think of my paunch, which is more
　　pronounced.
You are a little spoon.

You curve, curve, curve.

You need to speak more loudly to be heard above the
  creek.

Your red flannel on the gold upholstery somehow matches.

You say a little prayer for you.

You stay very still, like a lark silent in grass, after you wake.

You dab your forehead and the handkerchief is still dry.

You are the peach in the corner of my eye.

You fasten your suspenders and head to the jamboree.

You wake me with your heavy breath.

You grow your beard.

You settle the way good wine settles in a glass, with legs.

You paste your face on a picture of the Queen.

You are a sack of it.

You never smoke but there I find you, on the deck.

You reinvent naked by acting as though you are not.

You lean over the sink, a slight curve in your back, teasing
  your hair.

Your scarf hangs untied, like it wants me to tie it.

Your legs expect a thank-you note.

You ribbon-wreath the room.

Your clothes maintain their shape for many months.

You glance up to the grand planetary alignment.

Your posture, in comparison to my posture, is superior.

You are all about.
You have two cheeks for weather to settle on.
Your back is pink like the world is slapping you
    congratulations.
You lean, are you going to kiss me goodnight?
You are prettier than I, prettier than I, prettier than I.

I have nothing to say to you today, but you keep looking
at me like that, like you're waiting for me to say something
to you. Were it the case that we never looked at each
other, we might also never talk. Or at least rarely talk, and
certainly not about skin, or the movement of molecules. How
unfortunate, that we can't just stare and stare some more,
looking at the *Object* without imagining our lips nestled in
fur. This dress fails to fit my form, a strap off my shoulders
and hips hidden. My body and the body suggested by
fabric are two pears, ripe and fallen from the same branch.
The whole tree, growing there above me. And when I look
up I want to climb it to the brittle, bending branches, fruit
shaken to the ground while I yell that you should catch one.

Bourgeois recovered old materials to make her *Cells*.
Shattered panes from Brooklyn, gazed from for decades
before we all peeked in. She "salvages" them, "reclaims"
them. I want to leave the old wood to rot but try to find the
best pieces instead. It was many decades before Bourgeois
was recognized as brilliant. She was in a shop, or a falling-
down warehouse. Toeing the planks and flipping them over.
Keep kissing me, you'll see, new houses aren't haunted yet.
I'm picking through all my old mistakes and offering you the
best ones, their blue glow like a hangover headache. Hello
ghost, I'm going to use you.

The impulse to run your hand along the wall, touching it but
so barely and forward. Sitting room and coats of paint. You
shake out the sheets. You disperse like a drying pond.

Had Man Ray photographed me, I would have thousands of proofs of my beauty, my ink-stained hands. I would not need to write you an essay. Yet Oppenheim went on, drawing and sculpting without notice. With all my past selves apparating around us like wall-hung portraits, I wonder which you will look at longest. One of me is sweating in their sleep, one wide awake and dry. Rita Bischof said Oppenheim's "clouds remain clouds even when they are cast in bronze and stand on a bridge." In my process of becoming, I hope you see me like a cloud, suggesting figures without becoming them. You can put your hands on my body and know I'm there, undelayed by the speed of light to your eye, and if I grow heavy I will break to raindrops through your fingers.

I once dated a bartender. A weekend routine, shots and hands and barely knowing each other. One morning, stoned and watching *Man Vs. Wild*, he said, "I love you" and so I had to break up with him. What I mean is, I'm worried I am going to say the wrong thing to you during our programs. So sincere, with the "so" drawn out, stretched across the sentence. In the background, Robert Herrick and Ernest Dowson and Edna St. Vincent Millay all compliment my skirt. In the forethought, Tracey Emin understands. I told him that he didn't love me, that there were all these parts of me he hadn't met, but who I am to say? I put a window in my house, high above where the bed will go. The sun shines through every morning. It would wake us and there would be the day.

While we sleep, our memories settle, consolidate. We thread our fingers through each cobweb and transfer it to a shelf. We stop thinking about what happened so that we can keep that moment with us. Using Emin's tent would mean spending very little time looking at the names, and many hours in the dark and with your eyes closed. Everyone you loved is here with us, but I am relieved to not have to give them a fleeting thought. After not sleeping for two days, a person will still remember a face just as well as before, but won't be able to say how or where they met. Art in a white gallery, as though context could disappear. I sleep better when you aren't in my bed, when your name is on the wall.

Unsatisfied with the sounds it made, we filled the ocean
with buoy gongs and wave organs. There, something of
use. Noises for the fish to hear. I've yet to know an absence
that wasn't also a relief. Thank god that didn't go poorly,
as I drop you at the train yard. I am dating other people.
You met them, we had drinks together. In a couple of nights
I am going to put my arm around him and he will not be
you, just someone who is not you. The geometric equation
to discover the true alignment of the moon had to be revised
several times, every point on the earth a different number.
Different ways to go about the same thing, and the moon
stayed constant. I want you back, another chance for relief.
I want to announce you with the tide.

Tall buildings like lines, like gray places to be. A criss-cross and a hatch, a knit way to get to you. The thought heavy and coming out of the earth, a titan tied to a mountain pillar.

You have spent years learning the ways he wants to be
touched, so you must touch me that way, too. Uninformed
that our bodies are not the same, each arm different than
the last. Time is a poor way to decide if we matter to each
other. The planets are so rarely in line, and when they return
to that position, every surface has been made new by lava
and ice. I have been a person who removes their tie and
asks you to stay. Today I felt the mattress cooling, opened
the windows only once I was ready. It's not hard to fling a
satellite away from our gravity, the difficulty is in bringing it
back, those thousands of objects circling the Earth. I have
bruises on my legs that show you were here.

My last boyfriend had a boyfriend and my first boyfriend
a girlfriend. I'm not trying for a pattern, but if you draw
back the lens far enough, everything will line up straight.
Planes of intentionality, an x radius and a y radius that both
know where this is going. I declare everything okay with a
gray banner and I mean it. All the problems I can find are
cheap dates, just a little liquor and we're getting down to
business. It's a comfortable couch, knowing which days I
can see you. When the right planets are in the right order
they are supposed to allow power, like maybe we can feel
something. A chance not just for you, but for so much more,
him and maybe some day another you. And before you
know it the planets are out of line again, speeding past
nothing.

Like all his vases, *Golden Ghosts* required incredible skill
and patience from Perry. The throwing and oiling and
glazing and stenciling are delicate acts, and many of his
ceramics shatter. The heat, meant to harden, instead breaks.
We must always put ourselves through a fire, not to prove
our strength, but to form it. I hope that you know that I hope
there is an end to this. Some day, when I wake up and look
at you and don't think for a moment of myself, I'll hold my
hand and not brush my teeth until the sun cuts lines through
the blinds. I'll have nothing to say and know that we'll talk
later. The flaws are also what draws Perry to ceramics.
"Sometimes I'm almost disappointed when things work
exactly like I'd imagined," he said.

I demand that you make those postcard illustrations of your fingers to send into the world, appeasing your enraged admirers. They will tack them to their nightstands and tape them to their cupboards. When we are together, I will know that someone else is enthralled by the small white calluses of your palm. You are always going to have been with your boyfriend three years longer than you have been with me. And I, single I, will always have been with you longer than any new person I fall for. Choreography is one way to articulate time, your body moving us forward. A finger tapping.

Why would I think your boyfriend and I should have
anything in common? I am a break from your life. You
a pendulum, he and I poles. The two dead ends of a
trail. Were being loved by the same thing enough of a
connection, we would all live in the harmony of the bugs
that alight our shoulders, the deer so faithful as to always
flee. I would rather be bonded like the dancers, come
together as a raw supply. Lifted on one another's back, then
parting ways, back again to our own dates and dinners.
"Some are and make others like them," says the Gospel of
Philip, "while others simply are." We need a purpose, art
or a politic, and instead are given your pretty body. I hold it
tightly until you make a sound.

Bronze is copper and tin. Copper, like the roof and the pipes, swirled in the coins in our pockets. Tin, like something you can bend with your hands. I, like the roof and the pipes, something to shade the sun and bring you water. Me again, waiting to be bent with your hands. Let's find the straightest train track we can, unobstructed by cart or curve. You'll run down one rail and he down the other, your high knees dainty. I'll watch you grow smaller and smaller until you meet in my vision as the same dot, until you disappear. If this were a dance we would call the gesture "reaching." Like everything else, we want the earth to give more copper than it has.

When critics speak of artists who are women, they often
speak of the artists as women, like it is something that takes
them and they are taking it. There's always whiskey in the
teacup, if you fill the teacup with whiskey again. When
critics speak of Grayson Perry, they often speak of the fact
that he works in ceramics, a medium without respect or a
market. I am having trouble seeing the difference between
noting the conceit that restrains someone and blaming that
person. I look lovely, even though this dress is not made
for my body, and you look like it is 1994 with that part in
your hair. Ceramicists learn their craft by forming, drying,
and firing clay so many times that they can make flawless
vases, pots that don't show the human hand. With Perry, the
cracks are intentional, which means he likes them, not that
he expected them.

I am trying to locate what occults us. Yesterday, I thought
it was residence. Tomorrow, I might let myself believe
complexion. Your beauty is bubbles I can pop with a
poke, until I see you laughing. It is a pane of glass over a
painting, and I refocus my eyes to see my reflection. When
you went home I was relieved of the need to shower. Think
of all I might be doing when you are not with me. I might
be learning Russian, or making small planes to soar off the
roof. There's really no saying. It's my Russian-speaking and
plane-soaring that occults us, I decide, lying unshowered
in my bed. Were we together all the hours of the days, you
would see me, complete, and what then? Our imagination a
shriveled sigh.

I have a lot of friends. Did you know that? A lot of friends.
And they all like to drink with me and they all think I'm
funny and they say "nice dress." I think you might turn into a
potted plant you are doing such a good job of not-listening,
of letting my steam escape. It's a problem, needing you
to love me for who I am when I am preoccupied tattooing
"flaw," one letter onto each knuckle of my right hand.
To enter Emin's tent, you need to kneel and crawl, like
you are begging or asking to beg. To spend more than a
minute with the work, you have to lie down. Critics call the
experience "debasing," as though we otherwise spend our
lives standing up. If I were a boy you would love me and
also, I am angry because you think I am a boy. Emin has a
tendency to speak of her art in a way that contradicts the
critics who champion her, incoherent rambling speeches
when she just wanted you to lie down in her dirty bed.

This is what it's about again, joy from someone else. It may rise from inside my red, red body, but I need a witness, a splinter that lets my hand know it can hold. The camera makes of time an audience, while dance makes of time a dying fish. To choreograph our story, I mimic the bonds of water, I imagine the weight of another moon. When I was very young, I would sing the highest notes I could reach, my eyes closed as I pictured the beauty of a woman on a stage. Eventually, reaching higher, my singing would become a scream. And you, how happy you must be, telling me about him and him about me. Over whiskey, I answer my friend that I get to see you monthly.

I've invited your boyfriend over for dinner. I have set the table like in *Cell*, just some hands for us to contemplate. Careful! I'll say. There's a glass orb on your chair. The domestic is a routine that conditions us to such intimate things, lets us live with our doubts and cruelties but not need to notice them. The lies I tell myself are the thick and dusty fabric of curtains. My conversation is going to be pixie dust in your boyfriend's eyes, so he sees that life with me is a plump peach he can pick any day. "And these hands," he'll say, gesturing to the hands. "Would it be alright if I touched them?" And I'll purse my lips to suppress a smile. And he will pause and then, getting it, laugh. By the end of the wine, his legs around my legs, we'll both realize where you came from.

Drift away, earth constellation. Rip the girl right out of
me, and take the boy with you, too. Ground me in what
everyone else sees. Our geometry, a pattern as everywhere
as daylight. Axiomatic.

Drawn, a tear duct might be mistaken for a tear. A statuette
for a ballerino, one boyfriend for the other. On first sight,
Perry's vases read as classic art. You have to look longer to
see them as different, to start to form a narrative. Dramatic
and drunk, I stand on a crate and point down at you.
"There aren't enough frocks in the world to make you love
me again," I say. And "What if I moved to Portland? What
would you do then?" Form and content are two slugs
fucking, their slime all over one another until they may as
well be one big twisting slug. Someone stomped on form
and content and now they are goo. Someone dropped
them into the water from too-high-up. I'd find it easier to
accept that you are ignoring my antics if you would just put
those sunglasses back on.

Ugh. Really? Gosh. Awful. This is where we are again, is it? This cheap Indian buffet and this two-dollar well special, the places we say are our favorite places. First I remember Lake Michigan and then I realize you probably like to be other places, too. Then it's the mirror, so clear since they outlawed smoking. I might be your somewhere else. We used to believe the heart couldn't heal, that we had to replace it, but now we have evidence of imperceptible cell repair, just a wink ahead of our constant state of decay. Lie still and perfect, pizza-eater, and some decade you might be well again. I go to Lake Michigan twice, maybe three times a year. In the summer I wade up to my knees and the sailboats are dots. In the winter, the dunes and the white-iced lake look like one sweep of snow.

I am going to have thousands of loves, and each will have a ghost of me. "It's more like an apparition," you say. I will apparate to everyone who has loved me so that it is like they still love. "I think the verb form is appear," you say. A ghost following someone who has moved on is needy, but an apparition is a holy experience, a blessing. I am sad sand rising and floating, so many parts to me that I seem to take shape. I am a face in a fireplace. Claire is drawn many times on the vases, so there is one Grayson Perry and hundreds of pretty, permanent Claires. You can place her on your end table and, in enough time, you will not notice she is beautiful anymore. You might even put flowers in it. When someone finally collects me, you are going to brag that you owned an original.

We aren't supposed to talk about some bodies, a rule that
Schneemann broke. To be so crass, so armpit frank, is my
best worst tactic. Passing the time, you let me tell you all
the places I will put my tongue to pass the time. Says the
Gospel of Truth, "You are this understanding that seizes
you," so we eventually lie together, you and me. All these
moments, with the sun so real and the night crossing oceans
toward us, they all pass unfilmed, true only while they are
true. If we are unable to talk about both of the dinners you
had tonight, the difference between one chest and another,
then I may as well be a senator's wife. Slap me or I'm
taking the pearls, I demand.

The telescope you buried in my gut registers this as a collision. Your boyfriend is talking and talking, more than he has ever talked before. And how would I feel, if I showed up? Largely unthreatened, as you already have me to deal with. The tent moths making their happy little homes, flying away from the brown-leafed tree. It's like Disney's own nature film out there, beavers cooperating and the rabbits look like they are dancing in the shrubbery. Here in the city, he is talking about beehives, your boyfriend, and I sincerely care to hear it. I offer him a beer and he takes it. Are you panicked somewhere? Pleased, like an upright cake? Other friends show up and we stop talking to each other. When I leave I wave goodbye to the whole group and make general eye contact.

Cloudy glass. Spread thin. The breath ice-turned again and again. The ocean reaching with waves, then pulled back into its form. You hold me the same as you always have.

My gut is tied in a trefoil knot when you look to me like that, like you're thinking of who I am. Let's start two exponential snowballs rolling. The first is all the people who fall in love with us, with you and me both. The second is who you thought I was every time you thought I was someone. Each ball taking on snowflakes and twigs, yeti and Swedish villages. Our love is huge and projected, you cannot stop it. I have thought of myself this way for so very long, how can I dare to stop? It will take ball lightning, an extreme makeover. I will have to clean the mirror. The snowballs roll up every witty thing I have said and every blemish, too, an avalanche impacting upon you like the domestic. The snowballs become a snowball. The snowball asks you on a date.

I want a scene like in the movies, you arriving home and me at the window, tossing your golf clubs out. "I'll be at my mother's! Don't even think of calling!" All the while wishing I could stay. But you'll need to marry me, before the divorce. You'll need to dab red wine off my lips before I meet your family, and I'll need to crush glass in a napkin. Today, the only reason we have to leave each other is each other, all the pretenses washed away in the flood of our maturity. What nerve, to engage me with open and honest conversation. What nerve, to touch my cheek. "However trite and dilettante the images I put on clay," Perry says, "the material would bring it, literally, down to earth."

I try to explain to my friend why we haven't all been together, at least once, to consider. I want to say that being alone is the only truth our bodies offer us, that this is the reason the dancers don't discriminate between flesh. They all fall, what else is there to do? The sky is big, bleary, dark, just like it has always been, no matter which way it all is moving. You have those stars on your ceiling, the ones that glow and are green. You are beautiful every night. When something seems like it is always true, someone must come along, reach into her body, and read one more story from a scroll.

"Please," you say, "just stop bringing up my eyelashes."
When Emin moves her tent public, it is still her tent. The
people that she slept with, and we don't know what they
might have said to each other, names so impersonal. A
tent out in the woods, so you can move it if anyone comes
near. She doesn't find purchase on her experiences by
keeping them to herself, but by letting everyone comment,
the critics often noting her large breast size instead. Walls
and houses, beds and experiences I can or can't have. It's a
unicorn in the sense that it's a horse of confusion with a horn
of sincerity. It's going to stay in the corner of your sight, like
maybe you saw a shooting star. All up to you, high up.

You and I could never last, but with a third and a fourth, we have a chance. This does not make us worse than two that are always two. Fallen into the lake, I'll grab at you and you at your boyfriend, then I will grab at your boyfriend also and he, seeing that you are not being grabbed at, will grab at you, at which point whomever you grab, that person will sink in your arms. The bodies in *Meat Joy* writhe so wet. They don't care and just reach for someone who reaches back. Now be still like you just finished fucking. Now still like yoga is over. Now still like the rapture. And all the fish stopped swimming but the ocean still waved.

Look how easy it is to hate someone for being gorgeous.
You in your mink! With your eyelashes, too! I want to find
dinner parties and bring you there so people know that we
are together, that I must have quite the personality. Had the
Earth the view of a different celestial plane, we would have
a different cosmology, too. The myths we splay on the sky,
the beliefs to which we must adhere. With a second sun
to compare our star to, we would have known the holy is
flawed and dependent. Instead, we circled the same white
light and wrote it poems. I can't handle it anymore, all the
boys who try to pick you up, never knowing that you leave
tabs unpaid and rarely compost. Your boyfriend is calm as
a duck in a pond, like he has always known the sun and its
wavering reflection.

And how, then, do I tell if you love me? Your sigh is sharp again, as though that's a reply. In one moment of *Meat Joy*, the bodies' movement reads as joy, while the next, they wrestle one another without script. These moments are no different, an ecstasy emphasizing how pain is sacred. This is why the molecules of ice lose each other and drift apart. The most available recording of Schneeman's performance is actually three recordings spliced together, as one is always so many versions of itself. The while when we felt the same of one another, think of me as that person again, please, and I will think of you and your boyfriend as a tousle. It is impossible to track each dancer's motivation through the edits. At the end, while they toss themselves in paper trash, a girl group sings, "That's the way boys are."

Take your sunglasses off if you're going to leave. Look at me in the harsh light and remember every pore. It's true, I'm hideous, and what lovely qualities I must have had. What flaws of your own will. I'm going to the art museum today, the contemporary one where beauty is gauche. Someone is going to tell me a stool reminds her of Louise Bourgeoisie because we aren't allowed to sit on it and I am going to invite her to my bed. There is a spot I lick that makes you shudder, and when I lick it on her I know she will stay statue still. Your boyfriend is an atmosphere, there before me and remaining to sustain you now. How dare you sit on my body. I'm art. Look at me! I'm god damn art.

There is a certain power in going. It's possible, lost at sea, bobbing in your little raft, that hundreds of hummingbirds will pass by. Flittering noise and red, you would still be impossibly far away from land. Things have been good between us, haven't they? Outside of my spells. We just learned about the hummingbird migration recently, the magazine tells me. Someone waking up, the birds a gentle breeze, no way of knowing it's not a good sign. First I have to chase a deer, touch a lake, then it's back to my house. I'll settle for you thinking wistfully of me if it means we can talk on the phone sometimes.

The mechanics of the train frozen, we have to travel in
reverse to Chicago, adding an additional day to the trip.
The landscape becomes present in my periphery, instant
barns and hillocks, and is slowly pulled away. I want to
always travel like this, how life fills us without warning. How
it is when I realize you are a fading point on the horizon
that I finally consider what you mean. There is someone in
Chicago and I am excited about him. He kissed me in a tent
near a lake, and when he came into my vision like a rush
of boy you stayed in the same summer-blossomed distance.
Ohio has been flattened by winter and, seeing so far in
every white direction, I let my eyes settle on the all of it.

How many of us are there? How many times is something performed before there is a very real consistency to it, and how many times more? No one is naked in the film, just thin briefs and bras. It is an empty act to reveal everything. "It just seems so feminist," you say, "like in the 90s." But still I want a three-person bed some nights, enough space to sleep alone. Still I want us to be always slipping together in blue paint, everyone off-screen and the camera's steady focus. At the trail's dead end, I'll consider the brush before turning and heading back. If we ever finish performing, I'll look again at our bodies and surely something will have been accomplished.

Collections of Gnostic texts usually take care to stress that they are not authoritative, that there is no Gnostic text. Just treat it like some thoughts on our love, ignore the parts that don't work for you. I think it's odd, that we expect there to be a book, something to close and put aside. The grammar isn't there for me. This is how we are living, the air is clean and I am with someone who wants to be with me today. The earth is at once radiant and cooling. Everything I thought would happen has happened. Pause and consider but move on, you are with someone who wants to be with you today. It's good, our knowledge of each other is still there. No one has found it yet, so maybe we'll find it together.

Drop to the ground, dance on the table. Everything is imperfect, the way the holy recognizes us. It is only by being imperfect and beautiful, imperfect and holy, imperfect and us that anything can be complete. When I fall to the ground, you dance. When I look up at the sky from the hollow, it is so much farther away than it has ever been before and also richer with stars. This is called divine, meaning it makes sense in a way we can't understand, that it floats. Perry's vases include the background and the figures atop it, the pastoral and the personal, together but not. Marionettes running while a painted scene scrolls behind. We will keep driving our loves away until our loves stay.

Construction becomes quiet, the saw buzz and the bang, little white wisps that stop at my edges. We'll get used to most anything, at least enough to keep going. The will of the wisp. I want to poke a hole in my words so that people notice you are not here. Comfortable divots you could fill some day, if you wanted to. My mother sighs, my friends sigh. "You're so sad," they say. I'm not, I'm really not. The shadow of the mountain turns with the day, encroaching. When it settles on me I put the hammer down and walk to where it is still warm.

Clapboard siding. The tin-snipped roof and stripped wires.
Solid steady and landscape, sinking to the frost line. A dress
flutter hung on the ladder.

In physics, Mach's Principle states that the movements closest to our bodies are controlled by all the mass of the universe. Absent the distant cosmos, I would reach for you with new motion. The neutrinos would float undetected through us in a different way than they float undetected through us now. Think of all our forgotten pasts, the trees we climbed that are still standing or that have fallen. So many people taking the fruit of the field into their growing bodies. And here I am, near a house in the mountains, ignorant of so much that pulls on us. Illustrating the principle, textbooks usually describe a person spinning in a field, their arms lifting from their body as they watch the sky turn. See? I want to say. None of it was my fault.

ACKNOWLEDGMENTS

All quotes from Gnostic texts were found in *The Gnostic Bible*, edited by Willis Barnstone and Marvin Meyer, published by Shambhala. I also greatly benefited from reading *The Gnostic Gospels* by Elaine Pagels, published by Vintage Books.

Page 4: "An enormously tiny bit of a lot" is also the title of the book accompanying Meret Oppenheim's 2006 retrospective. The text was edited by Therese Bhattacharya-Stettler and Matthias Frehner.

Page 36: *Destruction of the Father, Reconstruction of the Father: Writings and Interviews 1923–1997*, Marie-Laure Bernadac and Hans-Ulrich Obrist. MIT Press, 1998.

Page 52: *Strangeland* was published by Hodder Paperbacks.

Jeanette Winterson, writing for *The Times*. 22 October 2005.

Page 53: *Portrait of the Artist as a Young Girl*, Grayson Perry and Wendy Jones. Chatto and Windus, 2006.

Page 56: *Portrait of the Artist as a Young Girl*.

Page 58: Interview with Mark Gisbourne in *Contemporary Visual Arts*, no. 20.

Page 59: Interview with the television series *Art 21*.

Page 60: *Meret Oppenheim: Defiance in the Face of Freedom*, Bice Curiger. MIT Press, 1989.

Page 72: *Meret Oppenheim: Beyond the Teacup*. Independent Curators Inc., 1996.

Page 79: *Portrait of the Artist as a Young Girl*.

Page 96: *Portrait of the Artist as a Young Girl*.

Thank you to Ryan Van Meter and Margaret Macinnis, to Amelia Bird, and to The Ugly Truths. I am indebted to the advice and support I have received from my teachers, in particular Ander Monson and John D'Agata. My mother is amazing. Thank you to my community of friends and to IDA. And, of course, thank you to those boys who might recognize themselves in the "you" of this essay.

Elyza Touzeau

T FLEISCHMANN was born in Michigan in 1983 and lived by the Great Lakes until attending the University of Iowa and completing an MFA in Nonfiction Writing. Essays have appeared in *Fourth Genre, Pleiades, Indiana Review, Gulf Coast,* and *The Pinch,* as well as in the feminist magazine *make/shift,* and have been Notable Essays in *The Best American Essays,* 2009 and 2010. A Nonfiction Editor at DIAGRAM, T has settled in rural Tennessee after traveling for several years across the United States.